107 Tips for the Marine Reef Aquarium

by Albert B. Ulrich III

http://SaltwaterAquariumblog.com

Author's Note

I'm passionate about all things fishy, but my favorite part of the hobby is helping others learn from the mistakes I have made and the things I've learned.

As far as my story--well, I've been an "aquarium-nerd" for a long time. I wear that badge with honor.

The first fish I ever had were freshwater fish. I got them when I was either six or seven years old. They were livebearing fish. Well, feeder guppies, to be specific, because I had a turtle. Usually, the turtle made quick work of the fish I added to the tank, but for some reason, he completely ignored two guppies. Guppies being guppies, it didn't take long before the female gave birth to live offspring, which blew my six-year-old mind.

In college, I studied biology under one of the best minds in the aquarium hobby--Dr. Wayne S. Leibel, expert in all things New World Cichlid. I was amazed by the volumes of magazines on Wayne's bookshelf, each containing an article he had authored. It was then that I had decided to be an author.

It wasn't until I was in my mid-twenties, however, that I turned salty...pun intended.

I started with a basic fish-only tank--crushed coral substrate, a few decorations and some damselfish, which I used to live-cycle my tank. I read everything I could get my hands on. The typical advice online was often confusing or conflicting. The information in books was academic and not approachable for the average person.

For filtration, I used an under gravel filter (yep, I was stubborn) and had major problems with "problem algae," namely cyanobacteria and dinoflagellates.

I battled with ich and bought reef-safe (which I didn't need) garlic-based 'cures' (which don't work).

Eventually, I got the hang of things, and I decided that helpful information about the hobby shouldn't be so hard to find, and it certainly shouldn't be hard to understand. When I started writing about the hobby in 2009, my goal was to chronicle my own journey, but also find a way to do what I could to make it easier to learn about the important things—and have fun doing it, without the need for a Master's Degree in marine biology.

I have a dry sense of humor, so if you read something, and it feels like I'm pulling your leg, I probably am. If you read something and it doesn't make sense, maybe I'm making a joke, or maybe I just can't write. Either way, please have a laugh at my expense.

This book is intended to be chock-full of the most important tips and tricks I've learned over the years. I wrote it while thinking to myself, "Self (that's what I call myself), what do you know now that would have helped you have more success, if you knew it when you started?"

The tips are organized (slightly) by concept, but they aren't necessarily intended to be read front-to-back. If you're inclined to skip around, go for it. With over 100 tips, I hope you find something here that you didn't already know or weren't really thinking about. If at least one of the tips resonates with you, the book should hopefully pay for itself.

I'm glad to have you as a reader. Thank you for reading the stuff I write. Writing is somewhat of a narcissistic endeavor, but without you there to read it, I would just be talking to myself, which might signal something more wrong than just narcissism.

Table of Contents

Starting Out

We have to start somewhere. When I look back at how I got started in the hobby, I have to laugh. My system was pretty terrible. I was using an old under gravel filter powered by air pumps. I had a single, 40-watt T-8 fluorescent light above my 75 gallon tank filled with crushed coral gravel, two pieces of live rock (live rock is expensive!) and struggled because I was stubborn and did things the wrong way. If you are just starting out in the marine aquarium hobby, here are a few tips you can put to use right away.

1. Patience is more than a virtue in the saltwater aquarium hobby, it is a requirement

I know the feeling. You bought your new aquarium and absolutely can't wait to set it up and put some fish or corals in it. Resist the urge to go fast. Patience is one of the hardest things to come by, in life and in this hobby. It might sound a bit preachy, but you need to have patience and you need to set up a plan before you jump right into things.

I have become more patient, over time, mostly because of things I have messed up. One thing that has helped me is a goal I have set for myself to be more systematic in approaching the things I buy. Rather than run out and buy something as a spur of the moment, I try to deliberately research and plan out my purchases. If planning and research sound boring or lame to you, try to find a mechanism that will work for you that encourages, or reinforces deliberate choices over spontaneous ones.

It would be disingenuous if I wasn't transparent that window shopping and discovering an amazing new coral or fish doesn't excite me and energize my enthusiasm for the hobby. It's part of what makes things fun. But I can also say that some of my biggest problems have arisen as a result of this compulsive shopping. If any of this sounds like you, try to find ways to put steps in place to make sure your latest purchase from the local fish store doesn't jeopardize all of your purchases to date.

The need for patience extends beyond curtailing your purchasing habits. If you are like me, you won't want to wait for acclimation, and you certainly won't want to wait for a monthly cycle in quarantine before placing the livestock in your tank. Try to identify those times when you have that, "I don't want to wait" feeling and have some patience. If you do, you will make fewer mistakes. Take it from me, a recovering compulsive aquarist.

2. Leak test your aquarium before set-up

A few years back, I constructed a heavy-duty shelf and set up two rows of tanks in my basement, because I wanted to breed a few species of saltwater fish. I drilled holes in the tanks and installed bulkhead fittings, but I didn't leak test the tanks before setting them all up and filling them with water. That was a big mistake. Two of the eight tanks leaked. They weren't rapid, flood the floor leaks; they were tiny, seeping leaks.

One leak appeared to be my fault because I didn't install the bulkhead properly. The other leak came from one of the corner seams. Don't get me wrong, it might have been my fault too, from rough handling or trauma caused by drilling the glass, but regardless of the cause, the tank leaked and I didn't catch that leak until a day or two after everything was plumbed, set up and running.

I tested the first two tanks I drilled, but after that, I was confident in my craftsmanship and assumed the tanks didn't leak. That was a big mistake.

Instead of being a block-head like me, I recommend you assume the tank leaks. Even if you bought a brand new tank. Even if the crew from your favorite aquarium installation TV show built it, even if it belonged to a beloved friend, whom you would trust with your life—assume the tank leaks until proven otherwise.

If you think about it, we aquarists are somewhat fickle. We demand a lot of our tanks. We want breathtaking visibility from almost every angle. We want unobscured views. As a result, aquarium manufactures have developed ways to hold the aquarium glass in place with thin plastic frames and beads of silicone. These engineering marvels we call an aquarium are great at holding water, but not so great at putting up with other wear and tear.

Assuming the tank leaks before you install it creates an important mental shift that perhaps borders on paranoia, but will serve you well. Who would knowingly put a leaking aquarium in their den where it could cause serious damage? Nobody.

Before placing the aquarium in its final location, temporarily set it up in a location that won't get damaged if (when) the tank leaks. Fill it with freshwater, dry off the outside and draw a line with an erasable marker on the glass to record the water level.

Check back on the tank periodically over the next day or so and look for any drips along the seams or significant loss of water. If you see any drips, dab them with the towel and check back again in an hour. If drips keep forming, it means you have a slow leak. Either take the aquarium back (if possible) or strip the silicone and re-seal it. If the water is leaking out of a crack in the glass, it is best to just get a new aquarium.

If you are inclined to view an aquarium filled half-way as "half full" rather than "half empty," this approach may feel uncomfortable for you, but it's a lot more comfortable than standing with wet socks in a puddle in your den.

---

3. Torpedo your tank when you set it up— really

I am not an engineer, but I do play one on TV. Well, actually, I'm playing one in this book now— but if someone turns this book into a made-for-

TV-movie (and what a movie it would be!), then actually I will be playing one on TV. Ok, actually an actor would be playing me, writing to you, but this sideways logic isn't really going anywhere, so let me get back to my point (is there a point?)

Glass aquarium designs are engineered under the assumption that the aquarium will be level and that the water inside will exert an equal force on all four sides at the same time.

If your tank is not level, the water inside the aquarium is not level and therefore is NOT providing an equal pressure on all sides of the glass. One side is being stressed more than the other. Problems aren't likely to show up right away, but over time you are going to stress the seams of the glass and you may have a total aquarium failure, which is a fancy way to say you may have a giant, catastrophic leak. One day, your tank may seem fine, and the next day it could be leaking out onto the floor. It just takes a moment, but before you fill the tank, take out a torpedo level (that's the kind you can get at any hardware section or store with the little bubble inside a tube) and make sure the aquarium is level before you fill it up.

---

4. Put your tank on a waterproof floor, if you can

If I had a time machine and could go back in time to speak to my younger self. I probably would have a lot more important stuff to do than communicate aquarium advice, but let's assume I covered all that other important stuff and then started talking to my younger self about my aquarium. I would tell myself to figure out a way to get some tiles, vinyl or other waterproof material, under and in front of my display tank.

I am always dripping and spilling water on the floor. The carpet and padding are undoubtedly a mess. I hope it hasn't damaged the subfloor. That would be a VERY bad day.

The challenge here is that once you have your aquarium all set up and in place, you may not be able to fix the flooring without some major rearranging of your aquarium. That is the situation I am in now. I'm holding my breath because I don't want to tear it all down and start over. Do yourself a favor and start out with some waterproof floor materials, if you can. Give yourself enough room around the tank that you can splash around a bit and just mop it up with a towel. Future you will thank future me.

While we are on the topic of waterproofing, it can't hurt to take a look at your aquarium stand, too. For one of my tanks, the bottom of the aquarium stand rotted out from years of wear and tear, drips and spills.

Spills, drips and leaks are going to happen, and they are going to collect in the lowest point of your stand. Over time, this moisture can rot the wood and you could have a problem on your hands.

I applied a coat of waterproofing paint inside and outside my current stand as an extra layer of precaution. If you have the choice between a solid wood stand and a particle-board or plywood material, pick the solid wood, as it will hold up better to the wet stresses.

---

5. Establish your biological filter before you add any fish or corals

Your biological filter is arguably the most important aquarium system you have. Your tank is not ready for livestock until you have an established and stable biological filter. You can buy an aquarium filter at the store, but you can't buy a **biological filter** at the store, because the biological filter is made of millions and millions of bacteria that turn toxic ammonia produced by the fishes and corals in your tank into a less toxic chemical called nitrate. The process of establishing your biological filter is called **cycling the tank**, and your biological filter is said to be ready for your first animal when the tank has **cycled**. The term refers to the Nitrogen Cycle, which is the chemical process by which the bacteria convert that ammonia waste into relatively harmless nitrate. Your aquarium is a harsh, unstable environment before it has cycled. Subjecting fish and corals to these conditions is inhumane and a recipe for trouble.

Here is how the Nitrogen Cycle works: ammonia waste in your tank serves as a food source for a group of bacteria. Those bacteria consume the ammonia and create a chemical called nitrite as a waste product. That nitrite is a food for a different group of bacteria that turn it into nitrate. Nitrate is a waste product, but also acts as a fertilizer for macro algae growth. You may be wondering, *where does the cycle start?* Where does that first source of ammonia come from?

Unfortunately, some people (and some fish stores) recommend you start with an inexpensive fish. That process is called **live cycling** and should be avoided at all costs. The ammonia that can build up in the tank will burn the gills of your fish and can even kill them. I don't want to get melodramatic here, but live cycling is barbaric. There is another way.

A more humane approach to cycling a tank is to place a piece of uncured live rock, a small piece of shrimp from a shrimp cocktail, or a pinch of aquarium food and let it rot in your tank. Either of those items will decay in the tank and jump-start the nitrogen cycle with a nice spike of ammonia to feed those beneficial bacteria that will establish your biological filter.

6. How to speed up your cycle

Being responsible does have its drawbacks. It takes time to properly cycle a tank and make sure the habitat you have created has a stable population of beneficial bacteria that will keep your tank water free from ammonia and nitrites. One way to be responsible and speed things up is to seed your filter with bacteria from an established tank. The beneficial bacteria from the biological filter live on just about any surface in the aquarium: on the glass, on the rocks, on the individual grains of sand and on the filter media and sponges protecting the return pump.

Ask a fellow hobbyist to squeeze out their sponge for you or give you a small scoop of sand and you can jump-start your own biological filter by transferring a population of bacteria from their tank to yours. The gross-looking brown gloppy water they give you will look disgusting, but it will help speed things along considerably.

If you don't have a friend in the hobby who can provide you with some of the gunk from their filter, there are some commercially available products. Search for 'live nitrifying bacteria' online and make sure you get the product for saltwater use.

7. It's going to take longer than it does for those guys on TV

If you got into this hobby because you watched a TV show where the gang on TV built two super-awesome and amazing aquariums in an hour, I have to warn you that it takes longer to get going than it looks on TV.

The first thing to keep in mind is that the guys on TV have a huge staff that works on the tank builds all at once, so unless you have that kind of skilled help, you will probably have to do the work of all of those people, sequentially.

The next thing to keep in mind is that it is television, after all. Through the magic of TV, they take hours and hours of video footage and edit it down to fit in the one-hour time slot. You can't get a real sense for how long the project is taking, but I can assure you it takes much longer than one hour.

Leave the 1 hour crash-course aquarium installations to the guys on TV. For your own tank, I recommend you take your time and enjoy it. After all, this is meant to be a hobby.

8. Add livestock slowly

On those TV shows, they generally fill the tank to the brim with fish right away because their client paid top dollar for the tank and because they are on TV and an empty tank doesn't make for compelling television. But remember back to the biological filter tips? As mentioned earlier, the biological filter is actually made up of millions of bacteria that eat the ammonia and convert it (in a two-step process) to nitrate. Well, the thing is, if your tank is already cycled, it only has enough bacteria to manage the waste that is in your tank— no more, no less. If you were to add a bunch of fish to your tank without taking some super-serious ninja-style precautions, you would crash the biological filter in the tank because you would end up adding more waste than the bacteria could handle and you could end up killing off those bacteria.

What you need to do is add livestock one at a time, and test the water over the upcoming days and weeks to make sure your tank is processing waste appropriately. Every time you add livestock to the tank, you will create a miniature cycling in the tank (a spike in ammonia, followed by a spike in nitrite, followed by a spike in nitrate). You should wait to add the next animal at least until your tank has stabilized again and there is no detectable nitrite or ammonia in the tank.

9. Use a timer to regulate the light cycle

Aquarium animals tend to respond well to predictable cycles. One of the most important cycles for the health and care of corals and fish is the light cycle. Probably the easiest way to ensure a consistent light and dark cycle is to set your lights up on a timer. The amount of time your lights are on and off is called the photoperiod. Many people run their lights for a 12 hour on/off photoperiod, but you can adjust yours based on when you want to see your tank go on and off and by how much light your livestock needs to thrive. This simple step will automate the light cycle and get you on the road to success.

General Advice

10. Sign up for the Saltwater Aquarium Blog Newsletter

A great way to make sure you continue to learn about what helpful aquarium articles and videos have been created is to sign up for the Saltwater Aquarium Blog Newsletter. I will send you helpful, interesting and amusing resources to help keep you at the top of your game and feed your aquarium craving. There is also a free gift just for signing up.

Sign up at:

http://SaltwaterAquariumBlog.com/Join

11. Give hermits enough empty shells or they will empty some shells for you

Even in an aquarium filled with expensive fish and corals, inexpensive hermit crabs can sometimes steal the show, quite literally. Hermit crabs are always in motion, walking around the sand and across corals, picking up food, detritus and algae along the way. By nature, hermit crabs are opportunistic eaters, which suits them well to aquarium life, because they will eat whatever tasty morsels your fish and corals leave behind. The giant shells they carry around on their backs make them adorable. Hermits need to carry around a shell, because unlike other crabs, hermit crabs do not have their own hard, protective shell —so they find a shell, climb into it and carry their home with them wherever they go.

When regular crabs get bigger, they molt and break free of their old shell. Their outer shell is soft (on a dinner plate, these are called soft-shell crabs) for some time until it hardens into their new outer shell. When hermit crabs outgrow their shells, they have to go find a new one. For that reason, you need to be sure to provide them with a few empty shell options.

If you have snails, and you don't give your hermit crabs empty shells, these otherwise docile opportunistic scavengers will take the opportunity to separate a snail from its shell in order to make its next home. In so doing, the hermit gets a new home and transforms the snails into evicted escargot.

---

12. Always have a lid and use it properly

Certain fishes, like flasher wrasses or firefish, are notorious jumpers. But the fact is that just about any fish can become a jumper if it gets startled.

Sadly, I have lost a few fish to jumping. Not just firefish and wrasses, but also clownfish and royal grammas. I have even had fish jump from a tank out of the small area where the lid was open, after I absent-mindedly left it open following a water change.

If possible, you should get a tight-fitting lid, and use it—all the time. You can use plastic mesh/screen if your tank is an open design, light diffuser (egg crate) or a polycarbonate or glass lid. Just make sure it fits tightly around all the edges and doesn't give your fish a place to squeeze through. Trust me, they will find a way to squeeze through.

13. Big fish eat little fish

One of the laws of the reef is that big fish eat little fish. My own rule of thumb is that I won't put two animals in the same tank if I know that one of the animals (a fish or shrimp) is small enough to fit inside of the mouth of the larger fish. The simple fact is that big fish eat little fish. Even if the two fish species are otherwise compatible, it's a fish-eat-fish world in there and I don't trust any of them to be on their best behavior, watching their manners. Don't put the temptation out there. Pass on that fish and wait for a larger specimen. An exception to this rule is often made with the cleaner species–which are generally allowed to go about their business, even though they would otherwise appear to be a tasty morsel.

One time, I fell in love with two awesome tobacco basslets. I brought them home, placed them in quarantine, watched and fed them there for a month before giving them the 'all clear' to acclimate them to the display tank.

A few hours after I put them in the tank, I noticed a flame cardinal, probably only 1.5 times the size of the basslets, sulking in a dark corner of the tank, behind live rock, with a giant 'growth' on its mouth. Upon closer inspection, I realized that the 'growth' was one of the basslets. The fish barely fit in its mouth. The head was still partially sticking out of the mouth, while the cardinal labored to breathe around the giant plug.

Big fish eat little fish, and many fish have surprisingly bigger mouths than you would think. The other basslet disappeared within the next few days. I think I know where it went. That was an expensive lesson.

14. Hawkfish are great beginner fish, but they don't mix with invertebrates

Hawkfish are a hardy group of fish that generally do quite well in an aquarium environment. They are predators that perch on the rock work or corals and watch for an opportunistic meal to float by. They are a favorite among aquarium hobbyists. There is just one draw back: they love to eat shrimp and crabs. Given the chance, they will even consume invertebrates much too large to fit in their mouths by smashing them up. You have to choose one or the other. If you choose both, you are really just choosing the hawkfish and an appetizer.

15. Don't expect to be a fish whisperer

If you want to keep fish like certain Butterflyfish, Angelfish, Rabbitfish or Wrasses, expect to have problems at some point. These fish are reef-safe for some or most of the time. Many people buy them and report success, but over time, instinct takes over and these fish may develop a taste for the corals or clams in your tank.

Don't expect to be a fish whisperer. You're not likely going to have success getting your fish to exhibit unnatural behaviors. If a fish you are interested in has a reputation for nipping at corals or clams, assume the fish will nip at the corals and clams in your tank. Assume the fish has expensive taste and enjoys nipping at the most expensive corals in your tank. Are you ok with that? If so, continue on your quest to keep these fish. If not, then it's probably best to go to YouTube to watch a video of these beautiful animals and leave them out of your tank. But don't count on your ability to be a fish whisperer.

16. Bigger is not always better

When I first started in the hobby, the standard advice was to purchase the biggest tank your budget could afford. For one thing, people who get into the hobby and really enjoy it often trade up and go for a bigger tank—so if you stretch to the biggest tank you can afford when you get into things, the logic, I suppose, is that you would be better able to grow into your aquarium that way.

There was also a commonly held belief that larger tanks were more stable or at least provided the average aquarist with more room for error.

In my opinion, bigger is not always better. I do agree that size has some benefits, but it also has a few drawbacks. Larger tanks are more expensive to fill, more expensive to run and require more work to maintain. Those drawbacks more than offset the marginal, invisible benefit of incremental stability that the relatively larger size provides.

There are endless possibilities for customization in this hobby. With enough time and money, you could build the tank of your dreams. But sometimes I see hobbyists get in over their heads if they start out with their dream tank all at once. A lot of people will recommend you buy the biggest tank you can afford (or fit in your home).

Rather than jumping right to the end of the line and starting with hard-to-keep Small Polyp Stony (SPS) corals in a 210 gallon tank, start out small and simple and expand your aquarium empire as you get experience and learn what elements you like and don't like about the hobby. Many people start with a fish-only tank and then progress to Soft Corals, then Large Polyp Stony (LPS) and then progress to SPS, often increasing the size of their tanks as they go.

The cost and maintenance requirements increase as the size of the aquarium increases, and the demands of the livestock in your care also increases as you progress from the basic animals to the more complex. Resist the urge to jump right into the deep end and get your feet wet in the shallow end first.

17. Don't touch the glass!

When aquascaping your aquarium and setting up your live rock, make sure the live rock isn't touching the glass. It is generally best to leave enough room for your arm, holding a scraper or a magnetic float cleaner to fit around, beside and behind your live rock. If you don't leave enough room, that section of the glass will quickly get gunked up with algae and debris and will become an eyesore. I have heard about hobbyists propping rocks up against the aquarium glass on purpose, to create a cave they could spy into and observe, but I have no doubt those caves are a mess of algae and debris. Feel free to experiment, but be prepared for some dirty, hard to clean glass if you do.

18. Look closely at your insurance policy and check to see what is covered

All insurance policies are NOT created equal. Don't assume you are automatically covered by your insurance policy if your aquarium breaks, the plumbing fails or if you have a power outage due to a hurricane or other storm. Some homeowner policies will cover the cost of the aquarium and damage to the home, or even harm to someone caused by the fish (like if the fish bites someone), but they will probably not cover the cost of the coral. Don't take my word for it: every plan is different. I recommend you check out what your own plan covers, so you aren't surprised in the event problems arise.

19. Getting to the root of the mangrove situation

You probably wouldn't think of stress and the aquarium hobby working nicely together, but they do. Mangroves are trees that grow in coastal (saltwater) soil environments, and they can be a great addition to an aquarium sump or refugium. Mangroves are a great compliment to a saltwater aquarium because they are hungry for the nutrient waste produced by the animals in your tank. The trick with mangroves is to hang or suspend them high above the sand so that the roots can grow down into the sand. This is practical, as much as it is fun to watch, because the roots are the only part of the mangrove that absorb nutrients from your tank water. The more of the root you have in the water, the more surface area you have to absorb and remove excess nutrients. It also makes planting a mangrove more fun and interactive.

20. Don't use inexpensive plastic tubs as a makeshift sump

Resist the urge to use inexpensive plastic tubs as a sump for an extended period of time. You could get away with using one in a pinch, but these tubs are notorious for bowing under the weight of the water, becoming brittle and eventually cracking and dumping the entire contents in your den, living room or wherever you keep your display tank. They may seem like a good deal at the time, but it is not wise to use them over the long-run.

21. Baffle micro-bubbles to get rid of them

What are micro-bubbles? Micro-bubbles are tiny bubbles in your tank that can give your aquarium water a cloudy appearance and can damage the fleshy polyp tissue of some coral species. If you have a micro-bubble problem in your tank, you can install baffles in your sump to create a bubble trap. Bubbles like to float up to the surface. Baffles work by exploiting this physics factoid to trap the air in the sump and prevent it from entering into the return pump area.

Save Some Money

22. Join an aquarium club

One of the best ways you can take your hobby to the next level is to join an aquarium club. The club's online forum serves as a base camp for you to meet new people, learn from the questions other hobbyists pose and get your own questions answered. You will typically find people with a range of experience in these clubs, from newbie to expert. Club meetings give you an opportunity to meet with some of the people in your area and share some of the latest and greatest information. Club membership is also a great way to get discounts to local fish stores and to pick up used equipment and some inexpensive coral frags from fellow hobbyists. Club dues can often pay for themselves almost immediately.

Another fringe benefit of clubs is that you can participate in something called a group buy. A group buy is when several hobbyists get together and combine their orders to get additional discounts and free shipping. You can usually get an outstanding deal from an online vendor by partnering up with a group buy.

23. Save the mesh from citrus fruit for fragging

My favorite method for attaching coral frags is the plastic container and mesh method. Where do I get the mesh? I like to save the food-grade plastic mesh that citrus fruit like clementines, oranges, grapefruit and lemons are often sold in. Reduce, reuse, recycle and frag on. If you want to learn more about fragging corals, check out my book, *How to Frag Corals*.

24. Buy your glue at the dollar store

Cyanoacrylate, also known as SuperGlue, is a commodity chemical that could be purchased in bulk—but what are you going to do with that bulk? It dries quickly and becomes unusable. Are name brand glues really worth it? Aside from the packaging, there isn't a whole lot of value left to deliver. So why overpay for a name brand commodity chemical? Get your SuperGlue where I get mine, at the dollar store.

Regular SuperGlue can be thin and runny, which can make a mess on your fragging table and make you more likely to stick your own fingers together. SuperGlue gel is a higher viscosity (thicker) SuperGlue that won't run. It is perfect for attaching coral frags and is my glue of choice.

25. Extend the life of your glue

SuperGlue dries quickly, which is good news and bad news. It is good news because it means you can put your corals back in the tank relatively quickly after fragging them. The bad news is that the glue in your container will quickly dry up and harden once you open it—and even the smallest tubes of SuperGlue seem to have more than enough for casual fragging. If you don't want to throw out the tube of SuperGlue gel each and every time you open one up, you can put the glue in the refrigerator. Make sure you don't have any drops of glue on the outside of the tube, or you might watch your SuperGlue become a permanent refrigerator decoration, but the cooler temperature inside your fridge will slow things down, so that the glue doesn't dry out so fast.

26. Make your own live sand and live rock

Live sand is aquarium sand that has beneficial bacteria and/or invertebrates growing in it. The biological activity from the organisms in the sand is thought to be beneficial for and stabilizing to your aquarium. But aquarium live sand and live rock can be expensive to purchase. The fact is that any of the sand or rock in an established aquarium would be considered live sand. The sand in your own aquarium will become live sand on its own, over time. You don't need to spend a ton of money to fill your tank with the good stuff. Save some money by purchasing regular sand. If you want to speed things up, give it a jump start by adding a scoop of sand from a friend's tank. The bacteria and invertebrates growing on that sand or rock will seed the sand in your tank and act as a starter culture that will colonize the sand in your aquarium.

Live rock is like a box of chocolates; you just never know what you might get. Some aquarists are delighted by a hidden coral they find, but others are devastated when they find a mantis shrimp or other nasty hitchhikers on board.

Sponges, corals and other creatures can decay and foul the water in your tank. To avoid these problems, most hobbyists will clean and cure their live rock in a separate container to remove all former life prior to introducing it into their tanks. But why go to all of this trouble? The value intrinsic in live rock is supposed to be the creatures living on and in the rocks, but since the risks outweigh the rewards, most of us don't take the chance.

Save yourself the hassle and some money and use dry rock instead of live rock. It costs less money per pound, and since it is dry, you only pay for the rock, not the water too. Establish the bulk of your aquascape with the dry rock and add a few live rock accent pieces for aesthetic appeal and to seed your dry rock. Before long, it will all be live rock anyway.

27. Cheap rarely means a good deal in the aquarium hobby

Wild-caught fish often have a list price that is lower than aquacultured fish because aquacultured fish are more expensive to grow. But wild-caught fish generally don't survive as well in our tanks as aquaculture fish. Your first instinct may be that a $15 wild-caught fish is a better deal than a $20 aquaculture fish because you saved $5, but if the wild-caught fish dies suddenly, it actually costs you an extra $15. I know that isn't the case every time, but it happens enough to know your odds are much better if you stick with aquaculture fish. A cheaper price doesn't always mean something is a better deal. I learned this lesson the hard way, several years back, when I was learning how to breed the Banggai Cardinalfish. I shied away from the sticker price of the more expensive captive bred fish, but suffered significant losses from the live fish. Don't repeat my mistakes. I'm not suggesting you pay any price asked, but I do advise you to consider the overall value of your purchases. A low price rarely means a good deal in this hobby. You tend to get what you pay for.

28. Time to chill

If your tank is running warm/hot, you may need to set up an aquarium chiller. But before you spend that money, I recommend you try this out first—get a small fan (or a couple of small fans). Set them up to blow air across the water's surface and/or across the equipment creating the most heat (like your metal halides). Sometimes that air movement is all you need to dissipate (spread out) the heat. Moving air across the water's surface should also have a beneficial effect on gas exchange (oxygenation) too.

29. Recycle RO/DI water

Running a Reverse Osmosis/Delonization (RO/DI) unit creates a lot of waste water. Rather than just pouring that water and money down the drain, save and reuse the wastewater you create with your RO/DI filter to water the lawn, your plants or even wash the dishes. The water may have some minor impurities that would keep you from adding it to your reef tank, but in the grand scheme of water quality, it is probably some relatively clean water, so don't waste it if you don't have to.

Shopping

30. Don't buy on impulse

Let's face it, a lot of what is enjoyable in this hobby is buying stuff (either equipment or livestock), putting it in our aquarium systems and watching how it works or how the livestock grows and interacts in our aquarium. Buying stuff is a big part of what we do (and why it is such an expensive hobby). But buying stuff on impulse can get you into trouble.

Resist the urge to buy on impulse. Bad things tend to happen when you do. I will start out with a practical reason to avoid buying on impulse: for starters, you probably won't get the best deal if you buy on impulse. The stuff we buy in this hobby can significantly vary in cost, depending on where you shop. If you buy on impulse, you are likely going to overpay for your purchase. Beyond the practical, financial reason for not buying on impulse, there is an even more important reason: you are responsible for the care and upkeep of the living creatures in your tank.

Buying on impulse is reckless because you may not know what you need to know about keeping that animal happy and thriving in your aquarium. You may fall in love with an angelfish in a store, but it's not until you do the proper research online that you discover the fish requires a special diet that includes sponges.

If you bought that fish on impulse, you sentenced it to die in your tank. I don't mean to be bleak, morbid or (too) preachy here, but I would simply like to reinforce that you shouldn't buy anything on impulse before you know how to care for it and you are certain it will fit in nicely with the livestock in your tank.

31. Begin with the end in mind

Author Steven Covey lists this as the second habit in one of my favorite non-fishy books, *The 7*

Habits of Highly Effective People. Try to be aware of this habit and deliberate about trying to apply it any time you are shopping for your aquarium. In Covey's book, practice of the habit is all about visualizing the results first as a way of programming yourself to create the path to achieve that result. In the aquarium hobby, it is even more important because your tank acts as a living, breathing ecosystem that grows over time and with the livestock you add. So you need to think about what your tank will be one year, three years and five years from now in order to make responsible choices for your tank today.

There are an unlimited number of examples, but let me start with one. If your end goal is to have a tank filled with Acropora and Montipora SPS corals, you probably don't want to add that Green Star Polyp colony right in the middle of the live rock today because that soft coral will grow over anything and everything in its path—and you won't be able to grow your Acropora and Montipora corals.

Similarly, if you want a pair of premium-priced clownfish, like Picasso or Platinum Clownfish, I wouldn't recommend you add that pugnacious damselfish when you start your tank because that $5 damsel may attack those clownfish down the road.

Begin with the end in mind and create a plan.

---

32. Stash a cooler in your car

Unless you live in a location where it is constantly 78-80 degrees Fahrenheit, consider stashing a cooler in your garage or your car that you use for transporting livestock back from your local fish store. You don't want the trip home to be any more stressful for your fish or corals than it has to be. A cooler can help slow down the change in temperature of the water. Now, I don't recommend you stash the cooler in your car if you're the type of person who is inclined to make a bad choice (pick an incompatible fish or a species of coral you don't know how to care for), but if you only plan to pick up livestock you understand and have an adequate system to care for them, this tip can help you care for that livestock even better, so you aren't caught unprepared. If you do live in a place where it is constantly 78-80 degrees Fahrenheit, can I come visit? It sounds nice there.

33. Hand warmers are good for warming up coolers

Pick up a few packs of hand warmers in the hunting or fishing section of your local mega-mart or sporting goods store. Around here, a two-pack of hand warmers sells for just a dollar or two. What I like most about these hand warmers is that they are ready to produce heat on demand. They will last a long time, unopened, in your car or garage. Just rip open the bag to expose the pouch to the air, and the chemicals inside the bag react with the air to release heat. Tape that warmer to the inside lid of your cooler to create tropical temperatures inside the cooler and keep your livestock from getting too cold on the way home from your local fish store. This is overkill on warm days or with small coolers, but it might be just the trick on extremely cold days or with moderately sized coolers.

Best Practices

34. Set up a quarantine tank

One of the best things you can do to help maintain a healthy saltwater aquarium is to set up and use a quarantine tank. A quarantine tank is a separate, relatively bare tank that is dedicated to housing newly purchased fish for an intermediate period of time. Any of the fish that you purchase could be harboring parasites or a pathogenic disease. The only way to prevent the new editions from infecting those fish in your display tank is to quarantine them until you are certain they are parasite and disease free.

A quarantine tank is especially necessary if you plan to keep live rock, coral or invertebrates. The reason is that most parasites are invertebrates—and the major ways to treat and kill the parasites will also treat and kill the beneficial invertebrates living in and around your live rock, as well as the coral, shrimp and clams you may have added.

Once the infection gets into your display tank, it is often very difficult to get rid of.

The quarantine tank serves multiple functions. It provides a:

—Physical barrier between your new fish and the display tank, preventing contamination in the first place

—Way for you to closely observe and monitor the behavior of the new saltwater fish out in the open

—Way for you to safely treat and remove any threats without the risk of harming any of your other livestock

—'Recovery place' for your newly purchased saltwater fish to eat, gain strength, and recover from the stresses of shipping and pet store display—and get ready to compete for food and shelter with the other saltwater fish in your reef tank.

Adding fish to a tank without the proper quarantine period is like playing Russian roulette with your fish tank. You can get away with it for a few rounds, but after a while the odds stack up against you, and your fish will pay the price. Let me assure you, next to the protein skimmer, the quarantine tank is one of the most important pieces of equipment you can purchase. The trouble and expense to set it up pales in comparison to replacing your saltwater fish, coral and other invertebrates, catching any survivors, breaking down the tank and setting up the quarantine tank (QT) anyway. Save yourself the life lesson I learned the hard way and spend the money to set up the quarantine tank right away.

35. Add a refugium

A refugium is a great thing to add to your aquarium setup. Think of the refugium as a nature preserve within the confines of your aquarium system; it's a small area set aside for macroalgae and tiny invertebrates to flourish.

Adding a refugium to your aquarium can provide the following benefits:

–**Nitrate removal**–macroalgae in the refugium will treat excess nitrates in the water like plant fertilizer, and the more algae you grow, the more nitrate you will export from your aquarium system.

–**Boost the population of beneficial invertebrates** in your aquarium– Tiny little invertebrates (copepods and amphipods) can be found in most mature saltwater aquariums. The problem (if you're a copepod or amphipod) is that they're a natural and highly nutritious food source for your fish, and the fish in your tank will eat any 'pods they can catch. A refugium provides an oasis for these tasty morsels to grow without being munched on. Over time, a certain number of these 'pods make their way into the display area of your aquarium and boost the biological activity of your aquarium (or become part of the food chain). Either way, that's a good thing.

–**pH balance**–Isn't there a deodorant with the tagline pH balanced for women? Sorry, that was a tangent. A refugium won't help you smell better, but it can help with the pH balance of your tank. Many people set their refugium light to operate when the rest of the tank is dark. When the lights are on, plants and algae (including symbiotic zooxanthellae in your corals and clams) turn light and carbon dioxide into sugar, releasing oxygen. This chemical reaction can actually change the pH in your tank. Without a refugium set up on the opposite schedule, the pH of your tank will vary between day and night. Setting up your refugium to be on when your tank is off can help balance those pH swings, making your tank more stable than it would be otherwise.

There are two common places to connect a refugium to your aquarium system:

1) Most aquarists with a sump prefer to dedicate an area within their sump as the refugium area, that way the refugium is connected directly into the aquarium's existing plumbing and actually looks and acts like a part of the filtration system.

2) Another popular and easy way to add a refugium to almost any tank is to use a hang-on-

the-back style refugium (hang-on-the-back is sometimes abbreviated HOB). You can get these from your local fish store or favorite online supplier.

36. Dip your corals before adding them to your tank

Fish aren't the only animals in your tank, and they aren't the only things susceptible to parasites and disease. The corals you buy can pick up parasites or infections during transportation or at your local fish store just as easily. You should quarantine your corals and dip them before adding them to the tank to reduce the risk of contamination. Resist the urge to just drop them in your tank. An ounce of prevention is worth a pound of cure when it comes to parasitic infestations. ReVive coral cleaner is a good product to use for these dips.

37. Label your wires to avoid guessing games.

I'm not sure what it looks like under your aquarium, but I used to have a disorganized web of black wires under my tank, zigging and zagging in all directions, headed towards the power strips. That was fine most of the time, except when it was time for maintenance or if one of the electrical devices was causing a problem. Then it became a guessing game to see which cord was the one I wanted to unplug. A simple fix to this wire mess is to use colored electrical tape to label the wires to take the guesswork out. This can become extremely important if you ever have to talk a friend, loved one or tank-sitter through the process of unplugging a malfunctioning device from your tank while you are out of town traveling.

I learned about this little trick from an episode of the ReefThreads podcast.

38. Watch out for cross contamination

If you have more than one saltwater aquarium in your house, take care not to cross contaminate the two tanks. Wherever possible, have a separate set of maintenance equipment (like gravel vacuums and specimen containers) to avoid the unintentional transfer of pests or disease. Most of the time, your tanks should be happy and healthy, so it could be an unnecessary precaution, but you only need to be wrong once to be really sorry.

39. Dose new additives slowly

When starting out with a new additive, it is a good idea to start out even slower than what is recommended by the instructions on the label. You never know exactly what will stress the corals in your tank—and pretty much any significant change in water parameters could be that stressor. It just isn't worth the risk. If you are changing something up in your tank, make sure you start out slowly to avoid creating a stress point. There is one major caveat to this tip. If you are dosing a medication like an antibiotic or copper in your quarantine tank, you should follow the label explicitly because you have to ensure you are administering a therapeutic dose. In other words, my 'start slow' advice doesn't work with medication because you usually need a certain amount of that item in the water or it won't work at all. But if you are adding something directly to your display tank to boost the growth or improve the quality of the water, I recommend you do so slowly.

40. Give frags some time to heal before moving them

If you're going to trade coral frags with a friend, make sure you 'do the fragging' at least a few days in advance of when you plan to trade the frags. Fragging is stressful and your corals could probably use the time to heal and adjust to their new life. Oh, and feel free to ask your friend to do the same if they are providing frags to you.

41. Nets are best used for chasing fish, not catching them

If you have ever tried to catch a fish with a net, you already know they are smart enough to recognize the net and flee capture. The truth is that nets aren't all that good at catching aquarium fish. Even worse, using a net can actually hurt the fish. Use nets for what they are best at doing— scaring and chasing fish. Submerge a clear specimen container or other plastic container into the tank and use the net to chase the fish into the container. You'll have a better chance of actually catching the fish that way and less of a chance of hurting them in the process.

Maintenance

42. Use vinegar and a toothbrush to clean up equipment

Equipment gets "gunked" up pretty easily in this hobby. Coralline algae and salt can leave deposits on equipment, and invertebrates like tube worms can grow on all sorts of things, like powerheads and pumps, and can significantly affect their performance. One of my favorite tricks to clean equipment is to use a toothbrush to scrub the equipment and then give it an acid bath. Vinegar is a weak acid and will dissolve some mineral deposits. Dilute the vinegar with water and be careful to only submerge what you need to because this weak acid can eat away at power cords and other equipment if submerged for too long.

43. When in doubt, do a partial water change

One of the best, all-purpose things you can do to improve the quality of the water in your tank is to do a partial water change. If your corals seem a bit flat or otherwise unhappy, it is best to do some tests and see if you can figure out what the problem is, but you usually can't go wrong with a well-executed partial water change.

44. Don't walk away from a siphon

It can be tempting to multi-task while you are performing your aquarium maintenance. After all, water changes are somewhat mindless tasks, and it can feel excruciatingly boring to wait for the siphon to fill that bucket. Don't walk away from the siphon. You might be thirsty, or maybe you thought of that one thing you could get done while waiting for the bucket to fill, but I can assure you that stepping away from the siphon is a recipe for a wet floor. Resist the temptation, and stay with the bucket. I have had buckets overflow, hoses slip out of the bucket, and fish jump out of the open tank. Trust me when I tell you, not to walk away from a siphon.

45. Bigger is not better when it comes to standard water changes

A few smaller water changes are generally better than a single, large water change, when it comes to routine maintenance because smaller water changes improve the water quality gradually. If your schedule allows, try to break your water changes up into relatively smaller chunks.

46. Any water change is better than none

If you read that last tip and thought, *There is no way I am going to do that,* rest assured that *any* water change is better than none. So don't let that last tip seem daunting and be a reason for you to slack off on performing maintenance.

47. Desperate times call for desperate measures

When you react to something going on in your tank, take a moment to assess the situation and be sure that the way you are responding is consistent with the magnitude of the issue. Much of the time, it is best to go slow, but if you are faced with a serious issue, like a major contamination, don't be afraid to abandon that traditional advice and take decisive and aggressive measures.

A lot of what we do in this hobby is based on estimating the relative risk. When the relative risk of going fast is higher than the relative risk of going slowly, it makes sense to go slowly, but if someone accidentally dropped bleach in your tank, the risk from the bleach is much greater than the risk of rapid water change—so you would want to remove as much of the contaminated water as quickly as you could. Don't let canned advice get in the way of dealing with important issues quickly.

48. Set a timer, so you won't forget

When you are doing maintenance on your tank, use Google Calendar to send yourself a reminder when everything is finished, to make sure you don't forget to plug things back in or turn pumps, protein skimmers and heaters back on.

Go to **https://www.google.com/calendar**

Click the "Create" button

Title your reminder "Don't forget to plug everything back in"

Set the time for an hour or two from now

Select the "email" option under "Notifications"

The good news is that taking the extra step to schedule a reminder will help you remember, and even if you forget, Google will send you an email to remind you to plug everything back in.

49. Replace evaporated water slowly and carefully

Water will evaporate from your aquarium over time. When water evaporates from a saltwater tank, the salt and waste stay behind in the tank, while the fresh water evaporates. To keep the salinity consistent, you will need to add freshwater back to your aquarium to replace the water that has evaporated. Use high quality freshwater and add it slowly to an area of the tank (or sump) that will not shock or damage sensitive animals. Temperature, pH and salinity differences between the water in your aquarium and the water you are adding to the tank can shock and damage your corals. This is another time when going slow is usually best.

50. Rinse, rinse, repeat

Always rinse new media (like activated carbon) with copious amounts of freshwater before use. There are usually fine particles of dust that will cause a dust storm inside your tank if you forget to rinse your media or if you rinse insufficiently. Rinse your media thoroughly before adding it to your tank, so the dust goes down the drain instead of into your aquarium.

51. Never move an aquarium with stuff in it

Aquariums are designed to hold water in one place. They are not designed to withstand the pressure of water sloshing around or to have rocks or sand shifting about while in transit. Moving an aquarium filled with water, sand or rocks is a mess waiting to happen. Always empty an aquarium before moving it.

52. Dirty buckets make dirty water

Clean out your water change bucket before mixing your water. You are going to a lot of trouble and expense to remove dirty water from your tank and replace it with freshly made saltwater. Don't put dust particles and debris in your tank by using a dirty bucket. Clean your bucket first to make sure your water changes are of the highest purity.

53. Stressed corals can release toxins in the water

Corals sometimes release toxins when stressed. This can happen sometimes after fragging, or anytime something major changes in your aquarium. If you are changing something up in your tank or are fragging your corals, consider running activated carbon for a short period of time to remove any toxins from the water. Your tank will thank you for it.

54. Keep the outside of your aquarium glass shiny, clear AND chemical free

Don't use ammonia-based cleaners to make the outside of your aquarium glass sparkle.

Step 1: use warm water and a rag to wipe away any drips or salt creep. This step will leave you with a streaky, drippy, dirty looking aquarium glass, but it will remove the bulk of the buildup.

Step 2: use a small amount of clean water and a microfiber cloth to wipe the glass clean. Sometimes it takes a little bit of elbow grease, but with a good microfiber cloth, you should be able to get that aquarium glass clean and shiny without the need for any harsh chemicals.

55. Use a razor blade for that clean-shaven (glass) look

One of the easiest ways to keep the aquarium glass clean is with a floating magnet cleaner. You can easily clean the glass with these great tools without getting your hands wet. But if you have fallen behind in your maintenance schedule and you have some coralline algae growing on the glass, your magnetic cleaner isn't going to be tough enough. If you have algae build-up on your aquarium glass (NOT ACRYLIC), the best tool for the job is a straight razor blade. Hold the razor blade at approximately a 45 degree angle, push it along the glass and watch the algae shave right off.

Lighting

56. Switch to LED lights to save money

For most people, the lights are one of the most expensive, if not THE most expensive, parts of their aquarium setup. Lights are expensive to purchase, but they are also expensive to run. A 400-watt metal halide fixture uses more than $250 of electricity every year if you run them for 12 hours a day (at $0.15/watt). The relatively high ongoing cost of electricity makes switching to LED lights an enticing proposition. You can create a similar amount of light output while consuming a fraction of the energy by switching from high intensity lights like metal halide and VHO to LED.

57. There is such a thing as too much light

Too much light or too much light–too quickly, are two of the major causes of coral bleaching in a marine aquarium (that sure was a lot of too's and two's). If you have intense lights, it is best to start new corals off by introducing them at lower levels in the tank and reducing the photo period. Gradually increase the exposure over time to avoid burning or causing them to bleach. This is also a problem when switching out old, underperforming light bulbs for new light bulbs. Reduce the amount of time they are on, provide some shade or otherwise accommodate an acclimation period when making big changes involving intense light.

58. Old bulbs are bad. Get rid of them, but not all at once.

As aquarium light bulbs get older, the amount of light they produce declines and the quality of the light degrades as it shifts toward the red end of the spectrum. Red light can actually act as a signal to stop or impede coral growth. You are also more likely to have problems from cyanobacteria or other so-called problem algae when the lights are fading. Keep a log of when you last replaced your bulbs, change them out on a schedule and don't skimp there. Make sure you get rid of your old bulbs before they cause problems.

Read more here:
http://www.advancedaquarist.com/blog/red-light-negatively-affects-health-of-stony-coral

If your lighting manifold has multiple bulbs in it, you don't have to replace your bulbs all at once. Consider replacing them one at a time, evenly spread over a period of time. This will create a more gradual improvement/change in lighting quality that won't be as shocking to your livestock as switching them all out at once.

59. Wear gloves when changing the light bulbs

"Stuff" from your fingers, oils, grease and dirt are easily transferred to the outer glass casing on most light bulbs. This can distort or block the light or even cause the bulbs to shatter and break when they heat up (in the case of metal halide lamps). You're spending a lot of money to get the best lighting for your tank; don't diminish or ruin it with a sloppy, quick bulb swap out. Glove up and do the job right.

60. Think about whether you have too much light over your aquarium

Depending on how intense your aquarium lights are and how long you have them on, you may actually be stressing and burning your corals. That's not a joke. Why not try to scale back the amount of time your lights are on by 15 or 30 minutes to reduce the overall photoperiod and see if there is any effect on your aquarium? Save some energy and lower the stress in the tank. A great time to remind yourself to do this is during daylight savings time, when you may want to adjust your timers anyway to keep up with your new schedule.

Safety

61. Use a grounding probe to avoid electrocuting yourself

Every now and then, the electrical equipment in our tanks can fail and release stray voltage into the tank. Suffice it to say, stray voltage is not a good thing. There is a piece of equipment, called a grounding probe, which is often neglected, but should absolutely be included in every single aquarium build. A grounding probe safely channels any stray voltage so you don't get shocked. They are inexpensive and super easy to install.

62. Keep a list of the critters in your tank and the potential dangers

Every now and then there are news reports of how someone in the hobby gets injured. A lot of the time, harmful chemicals, like palytoxin, are thought to be the cause, when an unknowing hobbyist does something to cause the toxin to spread. But what if something happened to you and you couldn't explain it? Would a non-hobbyist friend know to suspect the zoanthids in your tank? It's a good idea to create a list of the critters you keep in your aquarium and let loved ones know where you keep that list, just in case. Odds are that you will never need that list. It's even unpleasant to think about it, but if you ever did need it, you might be glad it's there.

I learned this tip from an episode of a *ReefThreads* podcast.

---

63. How to remove glue from your hands

According to the Super Glue Corporation, the best way to remove Super Glue from those sticky fingers is with nail polish remover made from acetone. Add a small amount of nail polish remover directly to the glue on your skin. This should dissolve the chemical bond between the glue and your skin and allow you to gently begin to peel off the glue.

For more detailed instructions, you can check out the information provided by the Super Glue Corporation:

**http://www.supergluecorp.com/
removingsuperglue.html**

64. Another example of why gloves are good

Always wear gloves when removing things from your aquarium. Tube worms and other critters will encrust the edges of magnets, clips or rocks and those tubes can really hurt your fingers when you grab them. I've jabbed more things into my fingers than I can count. It's not fun. My preferred gloves, if you care, are the Coralife Aqua brand gloves. They are made from a relatively thick and durable plastic that is perfect for picking up and moving live rock and coral frags without getting poked, prodded, pierced or punctured. The gloves are long and fit most of the way up your arm (shoulder length). In fact, I am ordering a replacement pair right now.

65. The importance of a drip loop

Water is great at doing a lot of things. One thing it is exceptional at doing is running downhill. For most of us, the electrical equipment we have in our tanks is plugged into outlets below the water level of the aquarium, so any water that gets onto the electrical cords tends to run downhill. You can cause some pretty serious damage if you get water into your electrical socket. Hopefully you have a GFCI circuit, in which case the only bad thing that happens is that the circuit trips. The best thing to do is make sure you create a drip loop with all of your electrical wires. A drip loop exploits the fact that the water wants to run downhill. With a drip loop, you create a bend in the cord so that the cord loops down below the socket and then travels back up.

If any water runs down the electrical wire, it will drip down to the bottom of the loop, instead of into your socket.

Dealing with Problems

66. Try hyposalinity instead of copper

Copper is often used as a remedy for parasitic infestations because it is lethal to a lot of organisms. Sometimes, copper can cause more problems than it fixes. For a chemical-free remedy to treating saltwater ich, try hyposalinity instead. Here is how hyposalinity works: by gradually lowering the salinity of the water in your hospital tank, you change the osmotic pressure. Larger vertebrates, like the hardier species of fish, are typically able to adjust to the lower salinity because they have complex organ systems that allow them to adjust to the osmotic pressure. Parasites, like marine ich, are not able to adjust to the change in osmotic pressure during certain stages of their life cycle and die in the process. For this reason, hyposalinity is often a preferred way to rid your fish of parasites without the need for toxic chemicals.

67. Prepare for emergencies

Stuff happens. It is a fact of life. The best way to handle an aquarium emergency is to be prepared for it. A few of the big issues can be easily anticipated. What would you do if your aquarium sprung a leak? How would you keep from flooding the house? How would you save the livestock? How would you keep the tank oxygenated and warm if the power fails? What would you do if a return pump fails in the middle of the night? Having a contingency plan for a few of these more common and predictable emergencies can help turn a disaster into a manageable problem.

68. React to problems, but don't overreact.

Fix small problems when they are small. Problems have a habit of snowballing in this hobby, so if you don't want to find yourself on the other side of the avalanche, it is generally best to fix problems as they come up.

The fair balance to the previous point is that you want to make sure you are addressing problems with the appropriate level of enforcement. You don't want to perform a drastic water change to address a tiny nitrate spike. You don't want to chase a fish for three hours, trying to catch it, to put it in quarantine because of a nicked fin. While I am an advocate for quick decisions and addressing problems right away, try to make sure your actions are balanced, appropriate and that the end justifies the means.

69. Leave super-sizing to the fast food chains

If you're having an algae problem, buy a cleanup crew that is appropriately sized to get your algae down over the long-run. Hermit crabs, snails and shrimp are great at helping you keep your tank clean, but if you buy a super-sized cleanup crew to fix an algae problem, that crew might run out of food once the job is done.

Instead of buying a big cleanup crew to get rid of the problem quickly, you want a crew that is appropriately sized for the <u>ongoing maintenance</u> of your tank, not a crew sized to tackle a huge problem quickly. If they run out of food, your crew may resort to other food sources (like corals, shrimp, snails or fish in your tank) or they may starve, die, pollute your tank and cause another wave of problems.

70. Redundancy is a good thing in the aquarium world

In the corporate world, the word *redundancy* is casually used sometimes to refer to an inefficient process. Redundancy is a good thing in the aquarium world. If you test your aquarium water and get a troubling result, make sure you clean your equipment and test it again (and again) to be sure. It is easy to get an inaccurate reading and you wouldn't want to overreact.

If you are installing an overflow drain in your tank, two drains are better than one. The redundant drain can help prevent a flood in the event of a clog. If your heater or a return pump breaks, a backup can help you get your tank up and running quickly.

If you are building a system for speed and throughput, you build it to be efficient. If you are building a system that won't fail, you build in redundancies. Think through the areas that could fail and build in a redundancy.

71. Having a problem with hair algae? Raise your magnesium level.

One of the common hassles in the hobby is hair algae. When this stuff gets a foothold in your tank, it can be a real drag to get rid of. One thing to try is to raise the magnesium level in your aquarium. This one step will help fix the chemical balance of your tank and may be all you need to tilt the scales in favor of getting rid of the problem algae. Keep in mind that this is not an instant fix. It can sometimes take time. You can read more about this on Aquanerd here:

blog.aquanerd.com/2013/01/magnesium-dosing-for-hair-algae.html

72. Lights out on problem algae

If you've done everything else right and are still having problems with cyanobacteria or dinoflagellates, try shutting the lights out for two days. Along with other maintenance like water changes and physical removal of the gunk, this can sometimes be what you need to tip the scales in your favor. When I set up my 92-gallon corner tank, I had some issues with dinoflagellates. I was doing water changes for a while and making a little progress, but it wasn't until I went lights out for a few days that I felt like I started to make significant headway.

73. "When you hear hoofbeats, think of horses, not zebras."

That is a quote from Doctor Theodore Woodward, professor at the University of

Maryland School of Medicine in the 1940s who was teaching a class of medical interns to be logical and systematic when evaluating patients to help counteract the natural tendency to jump to conclusions.

When you experience problems with your saltwater aquarium (and you will) remember the sage words of Doctor Theodore Woodward: "When you hear hoofbeats, think of horses, not zebras." If you do, the odds will be in your favor. Most often, the problems we face are of the garden variety, not exotic. Start with the most obvious solutions and work your way up from there.

Traveling

74. It's usually OK to skip a few days of feeding

I encourage you to take an unbiased look at the fish in your aquarium. Be honest with Uncle Al here. Are your fish overfed? If you are like the majority of us, your fish are probably overfed. If you have an established aquarium, your fish are healthy and fat, and you are planning to be away for just a day or two, don't worry about feeding your fish. They will be fine. We tend to have very regular, high calorie diets for our fish, and they probably don't get as much exercise as they would if they were in the ocean, so cutting back on some calories every now and then because of your travel schedule should be no problem at all.

75. Do your pre-vacation maintenance a few days before you go

Don't wait until the last minute to do water changes and other maintenance tasks, like cleaning out (and perhaps shutting down) your protein skimmer. I have found that problems arise more commonly after maintenance. Sometimes a powerhead comes loose or a protein skimmer overflows. The point is that you want to allow time for your aquarium to settle before you leave, to give any of those problems a chance to show their faces before you head out for an extended period of time. You will also be less stressed out before you go, because you can spend that last-minute time doing last-minute vacation prep instead of aquarium maintenance.

Disease & Parasites

76. Feed a bully, starve a parasite

Sometimes aggression between two fish is caused by a dispute over territory or feeding rights. At meal time, dominant fish are generally very active and feed aggressively, while subordinate fish often feed less. A great way to tire out a bully is to feed it multiple small doses and give them a full belly. They may be less likely to bother the other fish after this.

If you have parasites in your tank, like the infamous saltwater ich or flatworms, the best thing to do is starve them. Unfortunately, the parasites are feeding off of your fish, so the only way to starve them is to completely remove the fish from your tank. If you have coral-eating flatworms, you have to remove the corals from your tank. Without a host or source of food, the parasites left in the tank will starve and die while you medicate your fish or corals in a hospital tank. Once you are sure your display tank has remained fallow long enough, you can safely reintroduce the animals to the parasite-free tank.

---

77. If an animal can't be saved, consider removing it *before* it pollutes your tank

---

There are two competing schools of thought on how best to manage your aquarium when an animal is dying. On the one hand, you owe it to your livestock to try all practical means possible to keep them healthy and alive. On the other hand, you owe it to the other livestock in your aquarium to do what is best for them. That can create a moral dilemma. It may seem a bit harsh, but there are times when you will know that a fish or coral is beyond saving. Dying animals can pollute your tank. With corals, sometimes the death of one animal can trigger a chain reaction that could lead to the loss of several other coral colonies. If you know that an animal can't be saved, consider euthanizing it before it pollutes your tank. Just be sure to look up humane methods and do the best you can to be humane with the supplies at your disposal.

You have to decide for yourself, but consider figuring out where you stand on the issue before it happens, so you can make an unemotional decision when the time comes.

78. Disappearing ich doesn't mean you have won the war

Did that ich on your fish just disappear on its own? Think you're out of the woods? You may not be. Due to the lifecycle of this parasite, it may actually come back even worse than before. Appearing and disappearing infestations doesn't mean your fish are beating it. Ignoring the problem may give it time to get worse. Remove your fish from the display tank, and put them in a hospital tank where you can treat the infestation, while allowing your tank to go fallow in the process before reintroducing the fish back into the tank.

Feeding

79. Presentation is what makes food look appetizing

Presentation is what makes food look appetizing. This is as true for humans as it is for your fish. If your tang or angelfish won't eat seaweed from a clip, try wedging the seaweed into the live rock or attach it to a piece of live rock rubble with a rubber band. Sometimes this more natural presentation of the food is all the fish needs to figure out what you are offering them is a tasty morsel of food. In case you are wondering, presentation is only semi-effective with kids (at least with my kids), unless it looks like macaroni and cheese.

80. Clean food makes less waste

Lower phosphates and nitrates in your tank by rinsing your food before you feed your fish.

Frozen foods are good for your livestock, but sometimes the liquid your frozen food is packed in can pollute your tank. If you have a thriving population of soft coral species and/or a deep sand bed, this may not phase you, but if you are trying to maintain a low nutrient environment, you might be surprised at just how much that frozen food is polluting your water. Buy a reusable coffee filter and use it to thaw and rinse frozen food to remove the excess water and lower your phosphates and nitrates in your tank.

81. Turn off pumps and protein skimmers when feeding

One way to increase the amount of food your corals are able to eat is to turn off the circulation pumps during feeding time. This will keep the food suspended in the water column longer and give those filter-feeding or prey capture-feeding corals more time to grab a meal.

You may even want to plug the pumps into their own power strip, which would allow you to flip the switch and make it easy to turn off the pumps at meal time.

If you feed your tank at the same time every day, you could also put those pumps on a timer so they shut off and turn back on all on their own.

Some commercial foods can actually change the water chemistry enough to flood your protein skimmer, which will cause any skimmate to overflow and make its way back into your tank, polluting your aquarium water. Even if it doesn't overflow the skimmer, your skimmer will be working against you to remove nutrients from the water column, which is the equivalent of throwing food and money down the drain. To avoid the risk of overflowing the skimmer, turn it off. Just don't forget to put it back on when you're done.

82. Don't let the food manufacturers talk you into a portion size

While it can seem convenient that some frozen foods come pre-portioned in cubes, what are the odds that amount of food is exactly the right amount of food for your tank? Just because it comes out in one nice, convenient cube, it doesn't mean you have to, or even should, feed it all to your tank. You might be making your fish fat, and any uneaten food will pollute your tank. If you are experiencing problems with the nutrient load in your tank, take a look at the portion size you are feeding your tank and consider scaling back a bit. You can always refreeze any extra food and use it later. Better to do that, or even throw it away, than let it rot in your tank.

Picking Livestock

83. A tale of two corals

It was the best of corals, it was the worst of corals. If you have a choice between two corals in an aquarium shop, pick the coral with extended polyps over the one that doesn't and pick the coral that has encrusted the substrate or plug over one that hasn't. While not foolproof, these are signs of a healthy coral that has adapted to its environment. If a coral's polyps are not extended while you are in the store, it is entirely possible you just caught it at a bad time, but ask yourself how badly you want the coral and whether it is worth the risk.

84. Buy aquaculture first

If you have the choice between an aquaculture fish or coral and wild-caught always go for aquaculture. Fish and corals grown in aquaculture are accustomed to life in an aquarium setting. They generally suffer less wear and tear during transit to your local fish store, and are hardier and more resilient in an aquarium setting. Sometimes aquaculture fish and corals can cost more money than wild-caught, but they are almost always worth the premium price. You get what you pay for when it comes to aquaculture. Several years ago, I learned this lesson the hard way and watched several of the lower-priced wild-caught fish die because I was stubborn and didn't want to pay for the more expensive aquacultured specimen. Even though the aquacultured fish cost more up-front, they were a bargain in the end because they lived long lives, whereas I lost the total investment in the other wild-caught fish.

85. Another good reason for lights-out

If you buy livestock online, you may want to acclimate the livestock with the lights off. Those animals were traveling in a bag, in a box, in total darkness for at least the last day, so you don't want to blast them under the white hot lights right away. Give them some time to adjust. Acclimate them with the lights out. This will also keep your existing livestock in a relatively less active state, which should help your new additions out even more.

86. When acclimation may actually be more stressful to your livestock

Generally, it is advisable to acclimate your livestock to your aquarium conditions gradually, employing a process called drip acclimation. One thing to keep in mind, however, is that drip acclimation is intended to reduce stress to the organism. If the coral or fish your bought has been sitting in the same three ounces of foul water during a trans-oceanic trip from a wholesaler halfway around the world, leaving the animal in that foul water for a long period of time during a slow acclimation to your much better quality aquarium water may actually be more stressful than a quick fix. Just remember that while drip acclimation is usually good for locally purchased animals, you may not want to use it for animals that have traveled extreme distances or those you know are sitting in some pretty bad water. Remember that your best bet is generally to do what is in the best interest of the animal in your care. Evaluate every situation independently and pick the least stressful option given the individual circumstances.

Dealing with
Aggression

Unfortunately, aggression between fish in a marine aquarium is a common problem. Let's face it: a coral reef can be a tough place to make a living, and the fish we keep in our homes have evolved to survive in that fish-eat-fish world. When we pluck them off the reef and place them in their new home, it is only natural to expect a few scuffles along the way.

However, when scuffles turn into major aggression issues, serious problems can ensue. Harassed fish may become injured, sick or even die.

When it comes to aggression between marine fish, like many things in life, 28.3 grams of prevention is worth 0.45 kilograms of cure—or if you prefer—an ounce of prevention is worth a pound of cure.

87. Plan ahead

To prevent aggression between fish in a marine aquarium, the best thing to do is plan to add the fish in order of aggression-from the least aggressive first to the most aggressive last. Most aggression between fish is territorial in nature. The fish already in the territory tries to defend the territory from the new fish that has entered the territory. If you put the more mild tempered fish in the aquarium first, that will allow it to stake a territorial claim before the more aggressive fish is added to the tank.

In this way, you force the more aggressive fish to be defensive first and adjust to life in the aquarium once the territory is already divided up, rather than allow it to claim the entire tank for itself.

Of course, this little strategy is not a cure for mixing incompatible species, but it is certainly a great place to start.

One quick resource I like to refer back to is the compatibility chart from Live Aquaria. You can access that chart at:

**http://www.liveaquaria.com/general/
compatibility_chart.cfm**

88. Don't mix similar fish

As a general rule, it is not a good idea to mix fish from the same family. Let's say, for example, you absolutely love clownfish, but can't make up your mind which clownfish you want–adding a maroon and tomato clownfish into the same tank is a recipe for fighting and aggression. With just a few exceptions, it is best to stick with one fish per family, so take a moment to plan out your purchase–because you may have that fish for several years.

Aggression between fish is also common when the fish look similar, even if they are from different families. Try to mix species that occupy different areas of the reef with different appearances to avoid squabbles between similar-looking fish.

89. Add a cleaner fish to your tank

Another way to reduce the aggression in your aquarium is to add a cleaner fish. What is a cleaner fish? Neon Gobies and the Bluestreak Cleaner Wrasse are two species of fish that swim around the tank and pick parasites and dead scales off of your fish. Research has shown that the presence of cleaner fish in an aquarium diffuses the aggression in a tank. The more the fish exhibit this cleaning behavior, the more the aggressive behavior of the other fish is reduced. You can check out the scientific paper here:

http://beheco.oxfordjournals.org/content/ 19/5/1063.abstract.

90. You can't always judge a book by its cover

Just because a certain species of fish is typically known to be a peaceful community fish doesn't guarantee that the fish you buy will play nice in your tank. Every situation and every tank is different, so just treat this information as what it is: general guidance. Also, don't forget that, just like people, some fish are just jerks. I actually borrowed that idea from an episode of The Simpsons. You can watch it here:

http://youtu.be/JoAiyUduyrY

But it's true in life, elephants (that was what the episode was about) and fish. At the same time, don't think you can 'tame' a species that is notoriously a bully.

Change Up the Look of Your Tank

93. Get rid of those ugly frag plugs

Don't like the way corals look when they grow on frag plugs? Just because you bought the coral on a plug doesn't mean you have to grow it that way in your tank. Use your coral fragging skills to remove the coral from the plug and mount it on what you want, where you want, in your tank. Not sure how to frag corals? Check out the guide, *How to Frag Corals*.

Aquascape

94. Take time to plan out your aquascape

"Natural" looking aquascapes don't generally happen by accident or happenstance; they actually take some deliberate planning and structuring. You won't achieve your desired look by dumping the rocks in a pile or spreading the rocks out. I tried this a few times, with the intent of making a more "natural-looking tank," but the end result is a more boring looking tank.

What I have found is that the most attractive tanks are those with a carefully planned out aquascape.

You can always move things around later, but it will be a bit more challenging to do once your tank has corals in it. Take the time to plan your layout and rearrange it to get the right look when you first set up your tank.

95. Tell a story with your aquascape

Every great story has an attention-grabbing **beginning**, a **middle**, where the majority of the story building takes place, and a memorable **ending**–sometimes even a cliff-hanger. Beautiful aquascapes do the same; they tell a story.

The beginning of the aquascape story starts with a focal point. This is the area your eye is drawn to first. That focal point then leads you to the middle or body of the aquascape, and then finally the lines of sight take you to the end. If you want a breathtaking aquascape, keep this in mind and make sure your tank draws you in and tells a story.

96. Create openness and depth by keeping the glass clean

Grime, gunk, dirt, salt creep or algae on the glass can affect the look of your aquascape in a few ways. For starters, dirty glass makes the tank look dirty. If the glass behind and next to your carefully aquascaped rock-work is covered in algae (something I'm guilty of from time-to-time), your eyes instantly recognize the aquascape as something that is framed inside a small glass box. If you keep the glass squeaky clean (even if just to take photos of your impressive aquascape), you can trick your eyes into perceiving an infinite depth, like your tank is a sliver of the ocean, instead of a pile of rocks in a glass box.

97. Resist the urge to cram your tank full of rocks

Another key to a breathtaking aquascape is to have interesting positive and negative spaces. In other words, you need the rocks, but you also need open water, or else it will just look like a pile of rocks. Out of all the concepts listed here, this one is admittedly hardest for me to implement, but as I've grown to appreciate aquascape, I've realized how important this tip is to really making your tank stand out. Too much stuff in your tank and it will look crowded or cramped. Too little, and it will look sparse and empty. The best aquascapes are designed to create positive and negative spaces to make an impression and tell the story.

98. Watch out for too much symmetry

One thing that can make your aquascape pop is to pay attention to the way you use symmetry. Symmetry is where you make one side equal to (or mirrored with) the other side. For some reason, I would always try to make my tank symmetrical. I started out by putting my rocks in a pile in the center, or if I decorated with rocks on one side, I felt compelled to 'even out' the other side.

Reef aquascaping ninjas abide by something called the rule of thirds. Loosely speaking, you want to have focal points about ⅓ or ⅔ of the way up (vertically) and across (horizontally). Rather than create a focal point for your eyes to zip to (and then away from), successfully using the rule of thirds to your advantage creates interest and draws your eyes across the aquascape.

Take Better Pictures

99. Clean tanks photograph better

Did you ever notice that the most amazing aquarium photographs always showcase immaculate aquariums? There is a reason for that-clean fish tanks take better photos. If the pictures you are taking don't 'pop' like those tank of the month masterpieces, take a look at your aquarium with a critical eye. Are there any wires or unnecessary equipment in the picture? Is your sand clean? Is your aquarium glass clean? Make sure the glass or acrylic is clean and free of salt, streaks and smudges.

I like to use microfiber cloths to make chemical-free, smudge-free aquarium glass. Be patient.

100. Go to where the fish will be, not to where it is

Wayne Gretzky, one of the greatest hockey players of all time, is credited with the quote, "I skate to where the puck is going to be, not where it has been."

Keep this in mind when you are taking your own aquarium photographs. It is difficult to get an outstanding aquarium photo of your favorite fish if you are chasing after the fish. Instead, try to anticipate where the fish is going to be, or where it spends the majority of its time, and focus your efforts (pun intended), on taking fantastic pictures of that spot. If you can do this, you can minimize all of those other factors that will negatively impact your photos and then snap the photo when the fish swims into view.

101. Be patient and try, try again

You can't rush a great photo. Great photo opportunities just happen, so you have to have a little patience and wait for the moment to happen. Don't bank on getting the perfect photograph in one shot. In this digital age, photographs are free. Waste away. That doesn't mean you should take shots haphazardly. Your goal should be to make every shot a keeper, but what you will find is that the more photographs you take, the more keepers you get. Taking great photographs is a game of numbers. Increase the numbers and you will increase your success.

102. Be a straight-shooter

One of the common problems when shooting aquarium pictures is something called *ghosting*.

Ghosting is caused by refraction through the glass or acrylic of the aquarium and is a result of taking the picture from an angle. To eliminate ghosting from your photos, you need to be a straight-shooter—literally. Hold the camera perpendicular to the part of the aquarium you are shooting. If you shoot at an odd angle, your images will likely get some ghosting in your image.

103. Be ruthless about reflections

Probably the biggest challenge when photographing an aquarium is dealing with reflections in the glass. Close curtains or blinds, and turn off other lights in the room and the television. That may sound like blasphemy, but don't worry, the TV is a forgiving deity. Change out of bright, reflective colors and position the camera as close to the aquarium glass as you can.

If you take these precautions, you will dramatically reduce the amount of reflection and should end up with better photos.

104. Use a rubber lens hood

One inexpensive camera gizmo that can help you take better aquarium pictures is a rubber lens hood. You want the flexible rubber style hood, rather than the hard-plastic tulip flower lens hoods, because you actually want to place the hood directly onto the aquarium glass. This will essentially eliminate glare, and the soft, flexible rubber material won't scratch the glass or acrylic on your tank.

The lens hood will only help you, however, if you are photographing something deep enough inside the aquarium that your lens is able to get it in focus. That makes the lens hood very powerful when partnered with a macro lens. Every lens has something called a minimum focus distance, which means you have to be taking a picture of something at least that far away in order for the object to be in focus.

105. Focus close-up

The deeper into the tank you are trying to photograph, the harder it is take a good picture. For your best shots, you want to get close up. To get those up-close shots, you want to have a macro lens. A macro lens will help you focus the lens when fish swim up very close to your aquarium. But macro lenses can be fairly pricey and are not for the casual photographer.

One way you could improve your close-up shots without buying a separate macro lens is to use a Macro Extension Tube. You can pick up a highly rated extension tube for under $15. Compare that to a macro lens costing several hundred dollars.

If you combine the rubber hood ($7) with the extension tube ($15), you should be able to focus on subjects pretty close to your lens without reflections and glare from the glass.

106. Turn off your pumps

When taking pictures of corals, turn off the pumps. With the pumps off, the polyps of your corals will be moving much less, which will allow you to get a sharper, more focused image.

107. Eliminate the shake

Vibrations from your hands will actually shake the lens and cause blurriness in your pictures. The key to taking tack-sharp photographs is to use a tripod and remote shutter release. It takes a little longer to set up for a photograph using a tripod, but it is worth it. The pros recommend getting a tripod with a ball-head, but they are significantly more expensive. You may want to ease your way in with an entry-level purchase. There are several models in the $15-$30 range that have a lot of positive reviews on some popular online stores. That's where I got mine and I'm not a photophile enough to notice any deficiencies.

A tripod is almost useless without combining it with a remote shutter release because your camera will shake each and every time you depress the shutter button with your finger. The remote shutter release allows you to snap the photo without ever touching your camera, completely eliminating the vibrations from your hands in the process.

Where to get more information

Thank you for reading *107 Tips for the Marine Reef Aquarium*. You can read more of my fishy ramblings at:

http://saltwateraquariumblog.com

If you would rather have my fishy ramblings sent right to your inbox, you can register for the *Saltwater Aquarium Blog Newsletter*:

http://saltwateraquariumblog.com/newsletter

About the Author

Albert B. Ulrich III has been an aquarium hobbyist for more than 25 years. He is the author of **www.SaltwaterAquariumBlog.com**, has successfully bred three species of saltwater aquarium fish and has been published in the hobby magazines *Aquarium Fish International* and *Aquarium USA* 15 times.

The New Saltwater Aquarium Guide: How to Care for and Keep Marine Fish and Corals

The New Saltwater Aquarium Guide *How to Care for and Keep Marine Fish and Corals* will help you build the tropical reef marine aquarium you have been daydreaming about.

With a good plan, the right equipment and the right knowledge, you can build a successful, thriving new marine fish tank or saltwater aquarium.

How to Frag Corals

Fragging is actually genetic cloning, which isn't exactly the same thing as 'breeding' corals, but it is close, and it is about a zillion times easier than breeding corals. Corals are genetically programmed to reproduce clones of themselves from just about any surviving piece of itself.

Could you imagine growing a duplicate version of yourself from a locket of hair or a discarded fingernail? That's the kind of stuff comic book heroes do, and corals do that every day without a Hollywood budget.

This book will show you how to frag corals for your marine aquarium with step-by-step instructions.

Acknowledgements

When I am not busy writing my books or blog posts, I enjoy reading what others write about the hobby. One of my own personal favorite blogs to read is *Aquanerd*, at blog.aquanerd.com. The author there, Brandon Klaus, has been publishing there since 2009. A non-aquarium related author I enjoy reading and listening to (he has a podcast) is Steve Scott.

I'm not the first person to write approximately 100 aquarium tips, or so. In 2013, Marine Depot published an eBook, *100 Tips for a Successful Aquarium,* and this person who went by the name *lion_crazz* published 101 Tips on the **saltwaterfish.com** forums in 2004 (that was a long time ago). I thought to myself, "I want to do that, too." This book was inspired, at least in part, by these authors, who have both focused on providing tips that an everyday reader would benefit from.

So why would you want to read this book instead of those lists? Well, for starters, I don't think it has to be an **either/or** decision. In the bibliographic section of the book, you will find the hyperlinks to these other references, where you can look them up and learn from what those authors have to teach as well.

I wrote this book to share my side of the story with you. I read those lists and felt like I had more to offer—based on everything I have learned, experienced and read in my years as a marine aquarium hobbyist. You will find some overlap across the various channels, but *good advice* becomes *good advice* for a reason, and it is worth reinforcing.

Please review this book

If you enjoyed reading this book and think others would benefit from reading it, the most helpful thing you can do for me is tell a friend and leave a review on the site where you purchased the book. Product reviews are important, because they let would-be readers know what to expect, but they also factor into the algorithms the retailers use to decide what books to display when someone is searching for a book. If you are like me, you probably don't write many reviews, but I want to let you know that the effort you take means a lot to me, personally. I read each and every one, so if you have a few minutes, please leave a review.

Made in the USA
Las Vegas, NV
09 October 2021

32046525R00090